All About Animal
Frogs

By Edward S. Barnard

Reader's Digest Young Families

Contents

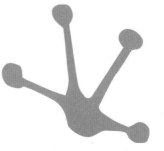

Chapter 1
A Frog Grows Up

Which is the male green frog and which is the female? The male's round eardrum behind his eye is larger than his eye. The female's eardrum is about the same size as her eye.

It is spring and the sun warms the water of a woodland pond. A male green frog is calling "Gungk...Gungk...Gungk" from a clump of grass at the pond's edge. He has attracted a female green frog, and she has laid her eggs.

The jelly-covered eggs float on the pond's surface. There are more than 3,000 of them stuck together in a gooey oval sheet. The eggs are smaller than the letter o on this page. As four or five days pass, the round dark centers of the eggs swell into tiny tadpoles, which begin to twist and turn and finally pop out of the see-through eggs.

One tadpole, just a little bigger than some of the other hatchlings, swims down to the muddy pond bottom. With his sharp, toothlike mouth parts, he scrapes off and eats bits of plants. As the days pass, the young tadpole grows large and plump.

Wild Words

Frogs belong to a group of animals called **amphibians** *(pronounced am FIB ee ans). Like fish, young amphibians breathe with gills and live in water. But as adults, they breathe with lungs and spend time on land.*

7

It is midsummer. The tadpole rests on the pond bottom. He is changing from a tadpole into a frog. Tiny hind legs are growing where his lower belly and tail meet. In a week or two, nostrils that are like the two at the end of your nose begin to form above his mouth. His mouth has widened into jaws that are beginning to stretch around his head. He once breathed only underwater with gills like a fish's. Now he has lungs, and from time to time he swims to the surface to gulp air. Front legs are sprouting from his belly. By late summer the tadpole still has a tail, but he uses his legs to swim. His eyes are larger and rise above his head.

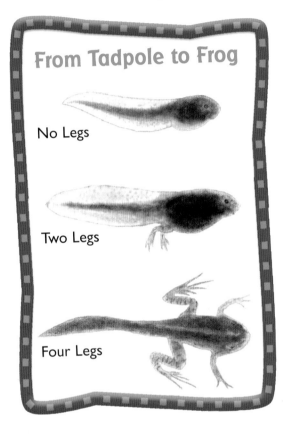

From Tadpole to Frog

No Legs

Two Legs

Four Legs

Not a tadpole anymore, the young frog suns himself at the pond's edge. The weather is getting cooler, and the sun warms him up so that he can move faster. He is cold-blooded. His body temperature changes with the temperature of the water and air.

The young frog has a very long tongue folded in his mouth. He will use it soon to catch insects. But he isn't hungry yet. He is getting all the nourishment he needs from his tail, which is being absorbed into his body. Only a stump is left, and it will be gone in a week or two.

8

A young green frog that has just transformed from a tadpole to a frog is small enough to fit on your finger — with room to spare!

Wild Words

Gills are organs that water-dwelling animals, such as fish and amphibians, use for breathing underwater. Most tadpoles' gills are inside their bodies and out of sight.

Green frogs get as big as they are going to get by the time they are five years old — about 4 to 5 inches from nose to rump.

It is now late summer. The young frog's tail has totally disappeared. He is hungry and often leaves the water to hunt in the grass along the pond's marshy shore. Whenever he sees something small moving near him, he shoots out his long, sticky tongue and snaps the insect or spider back into his mouth. If he sees a larger animal that might want to eat him — such as a raccoon, bird, or snake — he screeches, hops back into the water, and quickly swims away!

As the days become cooler, the young frog looks for a place to spend the winter. He swims to the bottom of a small stream flowing out of the pond. He finds a soft spot on the bottom and burrows partway into the mud. His heart slows down, and he goes to sleep. He will absorb the small amount of air

Keep Out!

Male green frogs station themselves along the edges of ponds in shallow water. Each male patrols a territory ranging from 3 feet wide to more than 12 feet wide. Males advertise their presence to females and warn other males to stay away by calling out again and again from various places inside their territories.

that he needs during the winter from the water flowing over his skin. He will stay on the stream bottom until spring, when the sun warms the water again.

Then the frog will swim to the surface, gulp some air, and head back into the pond to hunt for insects along the shore. In a year or two he will attract a female with his twanging call, "Gungk...Gungk...Gungk," and the cycle will begin all over again.

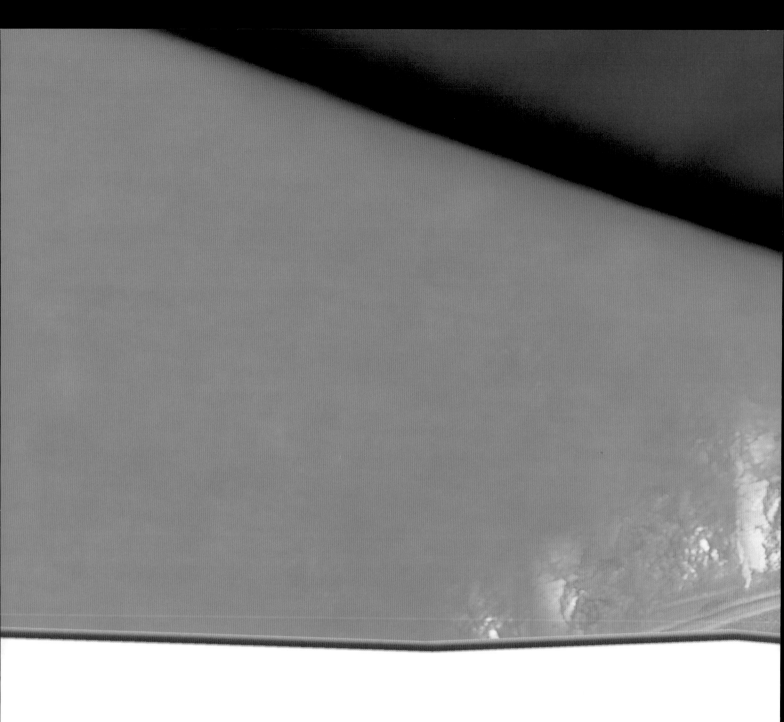

Chapter 2
The Body of a Frog

An American toad has drier, wartier skin than most frogs. It releases irritating juices from glands behind its eyes at predators.

Frog or Toad?

All toads are frogs, but not all frogs are toads. "Toads" is a word used for certain kinds of frogs.

Toads tend to have dry, bumpy skin. Frogs usually have damp, smoother skin.

Toads have plump, stubby bodies. Frogs tend to have longer, flatter bodies.

Toads have shorter hind legs than frogs.

Toads usually have unwebbed hind feet. Frogs often have webbed hind feet.

Toads don't have teeth. Frogs have tiny teeth.

Female toads lay their eggs in strings. Female frogs usually lay their eggs in clumps.

Toads live on land most of the time and return to water only to breed. Frogs live on land part of the time but may return often to water.

Despite these differences, sometimes only a scientist who studies amphibians can tell if a frog is also a toad.

Wet Behind the Ears

This young bullfrog's skin is damp and slippery. He climbs out of the water to sun himself from time to time but jumps back in when his skin dries.

15

Skin that Breathes

Frogs don't drink water. They absorb water through their skin, which is thinner than your skin. They also take in some air through their skin. They need this air in addition to the air they breathe in through their lungs. The skin of frogs sometimes feels slimy because it has mucus glands to keep it from drying out.

Frogs shed their skin as often as once a week or even once a day! They twist and turn to wriggle out of their skin almost the way you take off your sweater. Then they usually eat their old skin.

Skin to Hide or Warn

Often the color of a frog's skin matches its habitat so well that the frog is very hard to spot. Some frogs can even change their skin color to match background vegetation. A few frogs, like the Solomon Island leaf frog, mimic both the color and shapes of the leaves on the forest floor around them.

Instead of blending into their habitat, some tropical frogs stand out with wild patterns and brilliant colors that warn off predators.

Trick or Treat?

Brightly colored frogs are often poisonous, but some nonpoisonous frogs also use bright warning colors just to trick predators into looking elsewhere for a meal!

This South American frog's bright red-and-black skin says to predators — "Don't eat me! I'm poisonous."

A frog's ears are tuned to be especially sensitive to the calls of other frogs of its kind.

Why does a frog blink when it eats?

A frog uses its eyes to help it eat! As the frog swallows, its eyes drop through openings in its head. The eyes push against the roof of the frog's mouth and help force food down its throat.

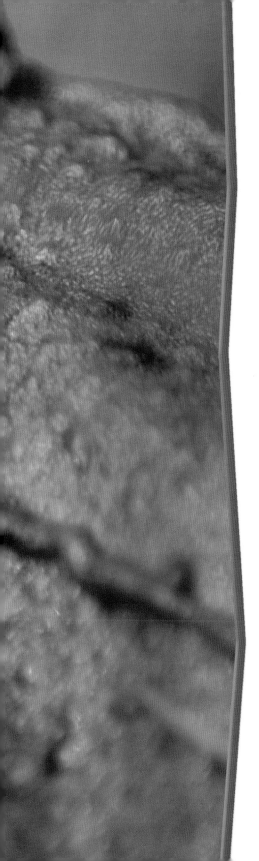

Eyes and Ears

A frog has a wide field of vision and sees things up to 6 inches away very clearly. Beyond that, the world looks a little blurry to a frog. But no matter how far away something is, a frog will notice it if it moves. If an insect stays still, a frog will ignore it. But if the insect flies, crawls, or wiggles, the frog will try to catch it with its tongue.

Most frogs have round, drumlike ears called tympanums (pronounced TIM puh nums) behind their eyes on each side of their head. When sound vibrates a frog's tympanums, they wiggle the frog's eardrums and send electrical impulses to the frog's brain. The tympanums also send vibrations to the frog's lungs. So a frog can detect sound both with its ears and its lungs!

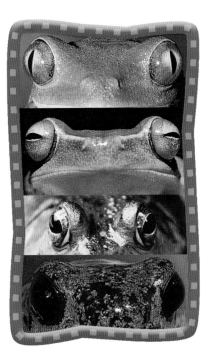

Eyes Unlimited

Frogs' eyes come in many colors and shapes. The colored parts, called irises, may be red, brown, green, bronze, gold, or silver. The pupils, the dark openings at the centers, can be slit-shaped like cat's pupils, round, oval, triangular, star-shaped, or even heart-shaped!

Frog Legs

Most frogs have strong, long hind legs, which they use for swimming and jumping. Frogs that spend most of their time in water have fully webbed toes on all four feet.

Some frogs that live in trees have webs between their toes that balloon into tiny parachutes when they glide through the air!

Other frogs that live in trees have no webbing at all. Instead, they have sticky pads on the ends of their toes to help them cling to tree trunks and branches.

Spadefoot toads have hard, sharp spurs on their back feet to help them dig burrows as deep as 3 feet underground.

Champion Jumpers

The longest recorded frog jump in the United States was made in 1986 by a frog named Rosie the Ribiter. At a fair held in Calaveras County, California, Rosie covered 21 feet 5 inches in three jumps. But a South American sharp-nosed tree frog named Santjie holds the world's frog jump record. At a South African frog derby in 1977, Santjie cleared an astounding 33 feet 5 inches in three jumps!

Some frogs can leap over 10 times their body length. If you could do this, you would be able to jump 50 feet or more!

Chapter 3
Hunting and Calling

23

If it moves, eat it!

Frogs and toads aren't finicky eaters. They will swallow almost anything that is moving and small enough to fit in their mouths, including mice!

The Great Plains toad eats grasshoppers, worms, and other insects that feed on crops. Its nickname is "the farmer's friend."

How Frogs Hunt

Tadpoles are usually plant-eating animals. They graze on the slimy green algae coating rocks, plants, and leaves on pond bottoms. But frogs are carnivorous (pronounced car-NIV-or-us). They eat other animals, such as insects, worms, spiders, and centipedes.

Frogs hunt by sitting and waiting until their prey comes to them. When a meal such as a dragonfly zooms within range, a frog opens its mouth and shoots out its long, sticky tongue, which is attached at the front of its mouth. It takes just a fraction of a second for the tongue to unfold, stick to the prey, and flip back into the frog's mouth.

Because a frog shuts its eyes when it shoots out its tongue, it must take very careful aim in advance!

Do Frogs Have Teeth?

A frog doesn't chew its meal. It swallows it whole. Toads don't have teeth, but some frogs have a ring of tiny teeth along the edges of their upper jaws and two hard toothlike bumps in the roofs of their mouths. These teeth aren't really for chewing. They're for holding wriggling things until they can be swallowed.

Frogs do not have throat muscles. They push food into their throats with muscles in their head and with their retracting eyeballs.

Calling All Frogs

Many male frogs make loud noises by squeezing their lungs while their mouths and nostrils stay shut. Air in the frogs' throats rushes over the vocal chords, and the loose skin under the jaw (called a vocal sac) inflates like a balloon. Vocal sacs make the sounds frogs produce louder, acting a bit like echo chambers.

A male frog sings loudest and most often in spring and early summer. His loud call is a warning to other males to stay out of his territory. But it is also an invitation to a female frog to come and lay her eggs.

Both male and female frogs make screeching sounds when they are disturbed by a predator. The sounds warn nearby frogs, who then jump into the water for safety!

High-Low, Fast-Slow

Small frogs have higher-pitched calls. Larger frogs have lower-pitched calls. The warmer the weather, the faster a frog will repeat its call. In cooler weather, the calls slow down because the frog's muscles work more slowly.

When the common European frog calls, it inflates two vocal sacs, one on each side of its head. Most frogs have only one vocal sac — located underneath the jaw.

Chapter 4
Surviving in the Wild

Frogs' First Cousins

When they are young, most salamanders live in water and have fuzzy gills sticking out of their bodies. As they get older, many lose their gills and develop lungs. Then they leave the water to live under rocks and dead leaves on the forest floor.

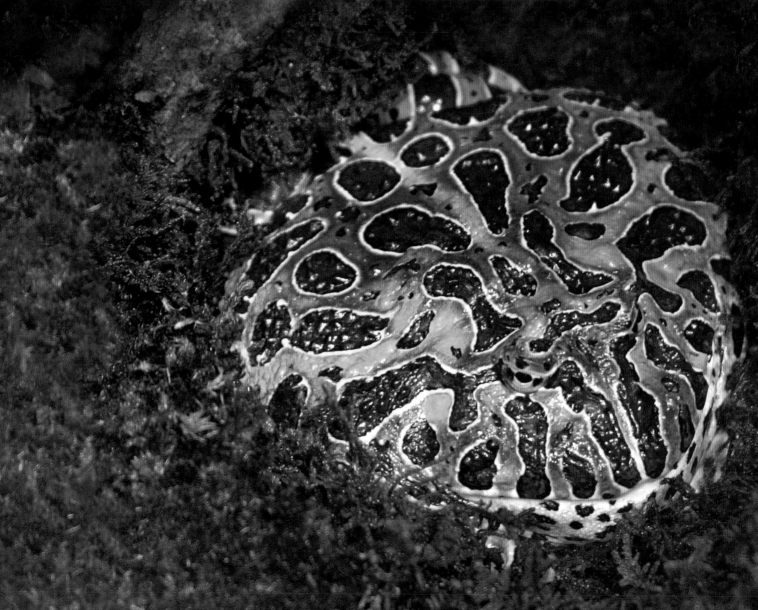

An Old, Old Family

Frogs have been around for a very long time. They existed even before most kinds of dinosaurs! A fossil of a frog over 200 million years old was discovered in Arizona.

The closest relatives of frogs are salamanders. Both salamanders and frogs are amphibians and spend part of their lives in water and part out of water.

Both frogs and salamanders are cold-blooded (their body temperature changes when the temperature of the habitat changes). They both have moist skin without scales. Salamanders look like lizards, but they are not closely related to them. Lizards are reptiles with scales.

A Frog's Life

Scientists have not found a good way to track individual frogs in their natural habitats to know how long they live. But scientists do know that frogs in the wild can live longer than those in captivity. Two examples are a European common toad that lived for 40 years and an African clawed frog that lived for 30 years.

Some people have kept records on the life spans of their pet frogs. Frogs in captivity usually live from 4 years to 15 years if they are well cared for.

The ornate horned frog is as wide as it is long and has a mouth nearly as wide as its body. Its nickname is "Pacman toad"!

Protecting Eggs

Many frogs lay thousands of eggs but then abandon them. But some frogs use a different strategy. They lay fewer eggs and guard them. One Australian female frog keeps her eggs inside her mouth. When her tadpoles hatch, they stay inside, living on their egg yolks. Once the tadpoles grow into froglets, the mother frog releases them.

The Surinam toad also keeps her eggs safe. She and her mate attach them to her back. Within ten days the eggs become embedded in little pockets in which the tadpoles hatch. Eventually the tadpoles transform into tiny toads, climb out of the pockets, and swim off.

Colors that Say Stay Away!

Some frogs have bright colors that protect them from predators. The red-eyed tree frog sleeps during the day. If disturbed, the frog startles predators by suddenly opening its brilliant red eyes.

When the fire-bellied toad is threatened, it arches its back so that its red-and-black stomach shows. If this action fails to stop a predator, the toad flips itself on its back, completely exposing its blazing underside.

Don't Eat Me!

A bad-tasting milky subtance oozes from the skin of fire-bellied toads. A predator that swallows a little of this nasty liquid and then spits out the toad is unlikely to try eating another toad with a red-and-black belly!

When a red-eyed tree frog opens its eyes suddenly, they say "Boo!" to predators and scare them away.

In Burning Heat

Frogs use some amazing water-saving techniques to survive in deserts. The Chacoan monkey frog has glands that produce droplets of waterproofing wax. Using its feet, the frog wipes this wax all over its body much the way you put on suntan lotion. The purpose of the wax is not just to keep sunlight out but also to keep water in.

Some desert frogs burrow underground in the fall and stay there until the spring rains come. They absorb moisture from the soil and recycle water from urine in their bladders. If the soil is very dry, they stop shedding their skins. The layers of skin build up around them, forming waterproof cocoons.

In Freezing Cold

Frogs can survive extremely cold habitats. The wood frog lives as far north as the Arctic Circle, and yet it doesn't freeze to death! When temperatures drop in the late summer, the wood frog burrows under leaves and goes to sleep until spring. Its liver produces a form of sugar that works like antifreeze in a car's radiator and protects the frog's body from ice damage.

When a Chacoan monkey frog wipes its body, muscles squeeze out wax from glands in its skin.

35

Chapter 5
Frogs in the World

This blue poison dart frog is less than two inches long, but its skin oozes poisons strong enough to paralyze or even kill predators.

All Kinds of Frogs

There are nearly 5,000 different kinds of frogs. Frogs live on every continent except Antarctica and on many islands as well.

The tropical rainforests are home to the greatest variety of frogs. Some tropical frogs live only in trees. Their eggs hatch in rainwater caught in leaves high up in tall trees, and their tadpoles transform into frogs without ever touching the ground.

Many tropical frogs, such as the poison dart frogs of South America, are brightly colored and poisonous. Native people tip their hunting arrows with deadly poison taken from these frogs.

Fewer frogs live in deserts than in tropical forests. Yet hundreds of different kinds of frogs can be found in the world's dry places. They often dig burrows or find other ways of protecting themselves from the sun's drying rays. A few kinds of frogs can even survive in cold places where summers are very short.

From Tiny to Tremendous

Frogs vary in size much more than people. The world's smallest frog is a black-and-orange frog found only in Cuba. It is about a quarter of an inch long — small enough to fit on your thumbnail!

The largest frog is the goliath frog of East Africa. It is 13 inches from its nose to its rear end, about the size of a small house cat. With its legs extended, it is nearly 3 feet long!

The Future of Frogs

Many kinds of frogs are endangered. They are losing their habitats as land is cleared for farms and houses. They are being killed by pollution because their thin skin easily absorbs poisons in the air and water around them. Also a deadly fungus disease is killing frogs in several areas of the world.

One of the best ways to help frogs is to join an organization working to protect the natural habitats in which these amazing amphibians live.

Fast Facts About Frogs

Scientific name	Bull frog	Rana catesbeiana
	American toad	Bufo americanus
Order	Bull frog	Anura
	American toad	Anura
Family	Bull frog	Ranidae
	American toad	Bufonidae
Size	Bull frog	4 to 6 inches long
	American toad	2 to 3 inches long
Weight	Bull frog	up to 1.4 pounds
	American toad	up to 0.2 pounds
Life span	Bull frog	up to 9 years in the wild
	American toad	up to 10 years in the wild
Habitat	Bull frog	Lakes, ponds, rivers, swamps
	American toad	Forests to backyards

One frog that is not endangered is the Cuban treefrog. Several years ago, it appeared in Florida, where it is now considered a serious pest. Besides insects, it eats other frogs and toads and tends to eliminate other amphibians wherever it goes.

Glossary of Wild Words

algae — tiny green plants without roots, stems, or leaves

amphibian — a cold-blooded animal with a backbone that usually lives in water when it is young, and on land when it is an adult

carnivorous — meat-eating

cold-blooded — having a body temperature that changes with the animal's habitat

gill — an organ that lets underwater animals breathe

gland — an organ that releases one or more substances

habitat — the natural environment where an animal or a plant lives

iris — the colored part of an eye that controls the amount of light entering the pupil

mucus — a thick liquid produced by body tissues, such as skin

predator — an animal that hunts and eats other animals to survive

prey	animals that are hunted by other animals for food	**territory**	an area of land that an animal considers to be its own and will fight to defend
pupil	the dark opening in the iris of an eye where light enters	**tympanum**	a round, drumlike ear behind each eye of a frog
salamander	a small amphibian that looks like a lizard	**vocal sac**	a pouch in a frog's throat that fills up with air when the frog calls
species	a group of plants or animals that are the same in many ways	**warning colors**	markings and bright colors on an animal that warn off predators
tadpole	a young frog with a tail but no legs that lives in the water and transforms into an adult frog		

Index